ZOE

Living in the *Fortified* Life of the *Spirit*

DR. JOHN ANIEMEKE

ZOE

Living in the Fortified Life of the Spirit

Paperback ISBN: 978-1-965593-79-0

Published by Cornerstone Publishing

A Division of Cornerstone Creativity Group LLC
Info@thecornerstonepublishers.com
www.thecornerstonepublishers.com

Author's Contact

To book the author to speak at your next event or to order bulk copies of this book, please, use the information below:

janiemeke@yahoo.com

Printed in the United States of America.

This book is dedicated to the BCAG Family
and the Body of Christ.

CONTENTS

INTRODUCTION

MORE THAN EXISTENCE

"There must be more than this."

I've heard this cry from countless believers over the years, faithful church members, tithers, worship team leaders, even ministry workers. They serve God, attend services, read their Bibles, yet something inside them whispers that there's a deeper dimension they haven't touched. A fuller experience they haven't accessed. A more abundant life that seems beyond their reach.

If that's you, I have good news: You're absolutely right. There IS more.

But here's what might surprise you: The "more" you're looking for isn't found in a new church program, a different ministry assignment, or even a more dynamic worship experience. The abundant life Jesus promised is already inside you; it was deposited the moment you were born again. The question isn't whether you have access to it, but whether you know how to live from it.

This book is about that divine life, what the New Testament calls Zoe, the very life of God Himself. Understanding Zoe changes everything. It's the difference between existing and truly living. Between religious routine and supernatural reality. Between being defeated by circumstances and being fortified by the indwelling presence of Almighty God.

EXISTING IS NOT LIVING

There's a detail in the parable of the Prodigal Son that never fails to arrest my attention. When the wayward son finally came home, his father said something profound: "This my son was dead, and is alive again; he was lost, and is found" (Luke 15:24).

Wait—dead? The boy was walking, talking, eating, making decisions. He had taken his inheritance, traveled to a far country, and squandered his wealth on wild living. He was very much alive biologically. So why did the father call him dead?

Because existing is not the same as living.

That young man had bios—biological life, physical breath in his lungs. He even had psuche—soul life, the capacity to think, feel, and choose. But he didn't have Zoe. He was separated from the source of true life, which is found only in relationship with the Father. Without that divine connection, he was merely surviving, not thriving. Existing, not living.

You can have money and not have life. You can have success and not have life. You can have a big house, a nice car, a prestigious position, and still be dead on the inside.

Don't let anyone intimidate you with wealth or status. Money cannot buy life. I've watched powerful people, people with billions of dollars receive a terminal diagnosis and suddenly realize that all that money means nothing. I remember one particular head of state, a man with seemingly unlimited resources and power, who one day was simply gone. All his wealth couldn't purchase one more breath.

But those of us who have Jesus? We possess something that transcends death itself. No matter what happens on this earth, we know we will reign with Him. Not only is that theology; that's the reality of Zoe life.

THE CRY OF YOUR HEART

Maybe you picked up this book because you're tired of merely existing. Perhaps you've been going through the motions of Christianity but deep inside, you know you're not experiencing what the early church experienced. You read about believers in the Book of Acts who turned the world upside down, who healed the sick, who rejoiced in persecution, who transformed entire cities and you wonder, "Why doesn't my Christian life look like that?"

Or maybe you're struggling with something that shouldn't have power over you anymore. An addiction you can't break. A temper you can't control. A fear that paralyzes you. A sin pattern that keeps repeating no matter how many times you confess it and try to stop.

If you're honest, you might be asking, "Is this all there is?"

The answer is no. This is not all there is. The Christian life is not meant to be a constant struggle with barely enough strength to survive. Jesus said, "I am come that they might have life, and that they might have it more abundantly" (John 10:10).

That word "abundantly" in the Greek means overflowing, excessive, more than enough, superior in quality. It's the picture of a cup that's not full but running over. That's what Jesus offers, not a trickle of life, but a flood. Not enough to get by, but an overflow that splashes onto everyone around you.

Let me tell you a story that perfectly illustrates what I mean by living beneath your inheritance.

Almost ten years ago, my cousin and I found ourselves in a massive penthouse suite in Bali, a luxury hotel we absolutely couldn't afford. A family friend had booked the trip but couldn't go, and the dates couldn't be changed. He didn't want the booking to waste, so he transferred it to my name.

But because we were broke students who had flown in from London, we were in full survival mode. I told my cousin: "Don't touch anything. Don't touch the minibar. We cannot afford this hotel." We ate outside like the locals. We lived on the complimentary breakfast in the suite—a massive spread every morning. We were literally saving bread from breakfast and eating it with Coke during the day. That's how cautious we were.

On our last night, we finally decided to eat at the hotel restaurant—just once. When the bill came, the waiter said, "Oh, you don't need to pay. You have points."

"What points?" I asked.

He explained that every day in the penthouse came with points, thousands of points, that could be used for restaurant food, room service, car rides, even massages. The expensive booking we'd been given included everything. The dinner we were stressing over barely touched what we had access to.

We started ordering everything—starters, mains, desserts. The table was full. We were full. The next day at checkout, they said, "You still have points. What do you want to do with them?" We ordered food for the road. They kept saying, "You still have much more."

At that point, I couldn't do anything more with the points. They had to go to waste. But I also couldn't believe that we'd spent the entire week living like paupers in a penthouse suite, not knowing we didn't have to.

As I walked out of that hotel, I heard it so clearly in my spirit: "Imagine being blessed and not knowing it."

That moment changed me. Because that's how I was living my life as a Christian. That's how many people live their Christian lives, saved but unaware, blessed but living like paupers. Not because God hasn't given enough, but because we don't understand what has already been given.

Salvation is not just a ticket to heaven. It's not just forgiveness of sins. It's a full inheritance. It's a complete package, identity, authority, access. But when you don't know who you are in Christ, you will keep living beneath what has already been paid for.

You pray from a place of lack instead of relationship. You beg for things that were already included. You live cautiously, afraid to touch what grace has already made available.

My pastor said it perfectly: "The revelation of the Father is the currency of the believer." That's our spending power.

Access is useless if you don't know you have it.

FROM RELIGIOUS LIFE TO GOD-KIND OF LIFE

For too long, many believers have settled for religious life instead of the God-kind of life. We've confused church attendance with spiritual vitality. We've mistaken theological knowledge for intimate relationship. We've substituted Christian activity for Holy Spirit power.

But God never intended for Christianity to be a religion; He designed it to be a relationship. A living, breathing, moment-by-moment connection with the Creator of the universe, made possible through Jesus Christ and sustained by the Holy Spirit dwelling within us.

This book grew out of a revelation that transformed my own ministry and walk with God. It began with two passages I couldn't escape: Galatians 2:20 and Romans chapter 8. As I studied, prayed, and wrestled with these scriptures, the Holy Spirit opened my eyes to something I had known intellectually but had never fully grasped experientially—the reality of Christ's life actually living in and through me.

"I am crucified with Christ," Paul writes, "nevertheless I

live; yet not I, but Christ liveth in me: and the life which I now live in the flesh I live by the faith of the Son of God, who loved me, and gave himself for me" (Galatians 2:20).

This is more than beautiful poetry, it's the operational reality of every born-again believer. The old you died. The new you is alive with the very life of God. This isn't metaphor; it's metabolism. It's not symbolic; it's supernatural. The same life that resurrected Jesus from the grave now pulses through your reborn spirit.

And that changes everything.

WHAT TO EXPECT

As you journey through this book, expect three things:

First, expect clarity. Many believers are confused about what actually happened to them at salvation. They know they're "saved," but they're not sure what they've been saved from or saved to. They know they're supposed to be "different," but they're not clear on how that difference is supposed to manifest. In these pages, we'll remove the fog and bring biblical clarity to what it means to be born again, what the new creation reality is, and how the life of God operates in a human spirit.

Second, expect transformation. This book is not meant to be read only. It is meant to be absorbed. The truths contained in these pages have power to rewire your thinking, renew your mind, and reposition your life. As you understand who you are in Christ and what you carry as a believer, something will shift inside you. The Holy Spirit will take these truths and make them real in your experience.

Third, expect impartation. I believe that as you read with an open heart, the same Spirit who inspired these words will minister to you directly. You won't only learn about Zoe life; you'll begin to live it. You won't understand it intellectually; you'll experience it personally.

This book is divided into chapters that build on each other, taking you on a journey from understanding what Zoe is, to recognizing how you receive it, to learning how to walk in it daily. Each chapter is grounded in Scripture, illustrated with real stories, and equipped with practical application, because knowledge without action is powerless.

My prayer is that by the time you finish reading, you'll no longer be content with existing. You'll be ready to truly live, fortified by the life of God, empowered by the Holy Spirit, and positioned to impact your world for the kingdom of God.

Your journey from existing to living begins now.

INTRODUCTION DECLARATIONS

"More Than Existence"

1. I refuse to settle for merely existing. I am called to truly LIVE with the abundant life Jesus promised.
2. The "more" I've been searching for is not found in programs or positions, but in the Zoe life already deposited inside me.
3. I am not defined by my circumstances, my past, or my struggles. I am fortified by the indwelling presence of Almighty God.
4. I declare that eternal life is not something I'm waiting for in heaven, it started the moment I was born again.
5. I move from religious routine to supernatural reality, from defeated living to fortified living.
6. I expect clarity about my identity, transformation in my experience, and impartation from the Holy Spirit as I walk in Zoe life.
7. I am no longer content with existing, I am ready to truly live, empowered by God's life within me.

1

THE GOD-KIND OF LIFE

Let's establish our foundation with Scripture:

"In the beginning was the Word, and the Word was with God, and the Word was God. The same was in the beginning with God. All things were made by him; and without him was not any thing made that was made. In him was life; and the life was the light of men. And the light shineth in darkness; and the darkness comprehended it not." (John 1:1-5)

Notice something important in verse 4. The English Bible says, "In him was life." But the Greek word translated as "life" in this passage is Zoe (ζωή). Not bios. Not psuche. Zoe.

Let's read it again with that understanding: "In Him was Zoe, and the Zoe was the light of men."

That one word, Zoe, is the key to unlocking the fortified life that God has for you. But before we can fully appreciate what Zoe is, we need to understand what it isn't. The New Testament was written in Greek, and the Greek language has a richness that sometimes gets lost in English translation. In English, we use the single word "life" to describe several different concepts. But in Greek, there are distinct words for distinct kinds of life.

Understanding these distinctions will revolutionize how you read your Bible and how you live your Christian life.

THREE KINDS OF LIFE

BIOS: Physical, Biological Life

The first word for life in Greek is bios (βίος). This refers to physical, biological existence. It is the life you inherited from your parents, the life sustained by food, water, and oxygen. It's the life that begins at natural birth and ends at physical death.

When Jesus spoke about the worries of this world in Luke 8:14, He mentioned "the cares and riches and pleasures of this bios." Bios is your earthly existence, your body, your physical needs, your temporal circumstances. It's the life that can be measured by a heartbeat and ended by disease or accident.

Bios is important. God gave it to you, and you should steward it well. But bios alone is not what makes you truly human in God's image. Animals have bios. Plants have bios. Bios is necessary, but it's not sufficient for the abundant life Jesus promised.

PSUCHE: Soul LifeMind, Will, and Emotions

The second word is psuche (ψυχή), from which we get words like "psychology" and "psychiatry." Psuche refers to your soul life: your mind, your will, your emotions, your personality. It's the non-physical part of you that thinks, feels, chooses, and expresses itself.

Jesus used this word in Matthew 16:25: "For whosoever will save his psuche shall lose it: and whosoever will lose his psuche for my sake shall find it." He's talking about self-preservation, about living according to your own desires and understanding rather than surrendering to God's will.

Your psuche makes you different from animals. You can reason, imagine, create, plan for the future, and reflect on the past. You have self-awareness and moral consciousness. But psuche, too, is not enough for the abundant life. Your soul was designed to be governed by something higher, by your spirit connected to God's Spirit.

ZOE: The God-Kind of Life

Now we come to the third word, and this is where everything changes: Zoe (ζωή).

Zoe is not biological life. It's not psychological life. Zoe is the very life of God Himself, uncreated, eternal, self-sustaining, and infinitely powerful. It's the life that existed before the universe was formed. It's the life that spoke galaxies into existence. It's the life that cannot be diminished, defeated, or destroyed.

When John writes, "In Him was Zoe," he's telling us something staggering: The Word (Jesus) didn't merely have existence, He had and has and IS the very life of God. And when that Word became flesh and dwelt among us, He brought that divine life into human reach.

Look at these descriptions of Zoe in Scripture:

- **Eternal:** "For God so loved the world, that he gave his only begotten Son, that whosoever believeth in him should not perish, but have everlasting Zoe" (John 3:16).
- **Abundant:** "I am come that they might have Zoe, and that they might have it more abundantly" (John 10:10).

- **Indestructible:** "In him was Zoe; and the Zoe was the light of men. And the light shineth in darkness; and the darkness comprehended it not" (John 1:4-5).

This is the life that Adam lost in the Garden of Eden when he sinned. This is the life Jesus came to restore. This is the life that's imparted to your spirit the moment you're born again. This is the life that makes you more than a religious person. It makes you a child of God with God's nature inside you.

WHY THE DISTINCTION MATTERS

You might be wondering why this matters. Why make such a big deal about Greek words?

It matters because confusion between these three kinds of life keeps believers living below their inheritance.

When most Christians hear "eternal life," they think of heaven; something they'll receive after they die. But that's not what Jesus taught. Listen to His words in John 5:24:

"Verily, verily, I say unto you, He that heareth my word, and believeth on him that sent me, hath everlasting Zoe, and shall not come into condemnation; but is passed from death unto Zoe."

Notice the tense: "hath"—present tense. Not "will have" but "has." Right now. Today. The moment you believed. You do not receive eternal life only when you die and go to heaven. Eternal life begins the moment you are born again. Eternal life starts from now.

This is crucial because if you think Zoe life is only something you'll experience in the future, you'll settle for just bios and psuche in the present. You'll try to live the Christian life in your own strength. You'll struggle against sin with soul-power instead of spirit-power. You'll exhaust yourself trying to be good enough instead of resting in the goodness already placed inside you.

But when you understand that ZoeGod's own life, is already inside your recreated spirit, everything shifts. You're not trying to become something you're not; you're learning to live from what you already are.

ZOE IS MORE THAN RELIGION

Here's something critical: You can go to church and not have Zoe. You can know the Bible from cover to cover and not have Zoe. You can sing in the choir, serve on the usher board, even preach sermons, and not have Zoe.

I'm not talking about church attendance. I'm not talking about being a good person or following religious rules.

I'm talking about being in Christ. There's a massive difference between religion and relationship, between being in church and being in Christ.

When I say you can go to church and still be lost, I mean exactly that. You can participate in all the external activities of Christianity while your spirit remains dead, disconnected from the Source of life.

Jesus said to the religious leaders of His day, "Ye do err, not knowing the scriptures, nor the power of God" (Matthew 22:29). They knew the Bible. They attended services. They prayed long prayers. But they didn't have Zoe. They had religion without relationship, form without power, activity without life.

That's why Paul could say with absolute certainty, "If any man be in Christ, he is a new creature: old things are passed away; behold, all things are become new" (2 Corinthians 5:17). Not "he should try to be new." Not "he hopes to become new someday." He IS new. Present tense. Accomplished fact.

The question is not whether you've changed if you're born again. The question is whether you're living from that change.

THE LIGHT THAT DARKNESS CANNOT OVERCOME

Look again at John 1:4-5: "In him was Zoe; and the Zoe was the light of men. And the light shineth in darkness; and the darkness comprehended it not."

There's a powerful truth here: Zoe and light are connected. The life of God produces light, illumination, clarity, understanding, guidance, hope. Where Zoe is present, darkness cannot remain. Where God's life flows, confusion flees.

The New International Version translates verse 5 this way: "The light shines in the darkness, and the darkness has not overcome it." The darkness has never overcome the light. Not once. Not ever. And it never will.

Simply put, No Zoe = No Light

If you are being overcome by darkness in any area of your life, if depression is dominating you, if addiction is controlling you, if fear is paralyzing you, if confusion is directing you, it is not because the darkness is too strong. It is because you are not drawing on the Zoe life within you.

You have the solution to every darkness the devil brings your way. You have Zoe inside of you. You have the power to overcome. The same light that conquered the darkness at creation now resides in your spirit.

The darkness in your marriage? It cannot overcome the Zoe light in you.

The darkness in your finances? It cannot overcome the Zoe light in you.

The darkness of disease in your body? It cannot overcome the Zoe light in you.

ZOE NOW AND ZOE FOREVER

One final truth before we move forward: Eternal life is not just about duration, it's about quality.

When Jesus talks about eternal life, He is pointing to more than the promise of living forever (even though that is true). He's saying, "You'll experience the quality of life that I have: the abundant, overflowing, victorious life of God Himself."

This means Zoe life is not postponed to heaven. It begins now. The moment you were born again, God's life entered your spirit. You don't have to wait until you die to experience it. You don't have to work for it or earn it or qualify for it. If you're in Christ, you have it.

The question is: Will you live from it?

That's what this book is about. Teaching you how to access and activate the Zoe life already inside you. Not striving to obtain something you don't have, but learning to release what you already possess.

In the next chapter, we'll look at how you receive this life and what happens in your spirit the moment you're born again. But for now, I want you to meditate on this truth: If you're in Christ, you have the very life of God dwelling in you right now.

Not a portion of His life. Not a limited version. Not a future promise. The fullness of Zoe: complete, unlimited, and unstoppable is yours today.

CHAPTER 1 DECLARATIONS

"The God-Kind of Life"

1. I have more than bios: biological life, and psuche: soul life. I have Zoe, the very life of God dwelling in my spirit.

2. I carry the eternal, abundant, indestructible life of God, the same life that spoke galaxies into existence.

3. Eternal life is not just about duration. It is about quality, and I possess that quality of life right now.

4. I am not trying to become a new creation. I am a new creation in Christ. Old things have passed away.

5. Zoe life in me produces light, and the light in me shines in darkness. Darkness has never overcome it and never will.

6. I do not live for God in my own strength. I live from the God kind of life already inside me.

7. The fullness of Zoe, complete, unlimited, and unstoppable, is mine today. Not a future promise, but a present reality.

2

DEAD MAN WALKING: THE NEED FOR NEW BIRTH

Without Jesus, you don't have access to Zoe life. Without Christ, you are merely existing, not living.

Some will say, "Are you trying to tell me that people who don't know Jesus as their Lord and Savior, who are enjoying life and living in the best houses—are they not living?"

Yes. They are existing, not living. They're not experiencing the best of God. It's only through Jesus Christ that we have life in abundance. We have eternal life. And that eternal life does not start when we die, it starts from now.

Any person who does not have Jesus as Lord and Savior is dead and lost. That's not harsh judgment; that's spiritual reality. There's a difference between being in church and being in Christ. There's a difference between religious activity and spiritual reality. There's a difference between knowing about God and knowing God. And until you cross that line, until you move from the realm of religion into the realm of relationship, you are in God's eyes, a dead man walking.

THE RICH MAN WHO HAD NOTHING

Let's go back to the story of the Prodigal Son. There's a detail here that should stop us in our tracks. This young man came to his father and said something that reveals the condition of his heart: "Give me my portion of the wealth."

Think about that for a moment. He's not asking for advice. He's not asking for wisdom. He's not even asking for a blessing. He's asking for stuff. Material things. Money. And the father, in his wisdom and grace, gives it to him.

The Bible says this young man took his inheritance and went to a far country and squandered it on riotous living. He had money. He had freedom. He had pleasure. He had everything the world says you need to be happy. But here's what you need to understand: You can have money and not have life.

A man's life does not consist in the abundance of things that he owns. Don't let anyone intimidate you with wealth or status. Money cannot buy life.

I've watched this play out too many times in my years of ministry. I've seen people with billions of dollars receive a diagnosis of stage-four cancer, and suddenly all that money means nothing. The doctors give them twenty days or twenty weeks to live, and they discover that wealth can't extend their breath even one day beyond what God has ordained.

I remember one particular head of state, a powerful man in one part of the world. He was a terror. He had all the money in the world. He wielded immense power. People feared him. And one day, just like that, he was gone. All the money, all the power, all the influence, none of it could keep him alive one more second.

But those of us who have Jesus? We have something that transcends death itself. No matter what happens here on earth, we know we will reign with Him. That's more than theology. That's not religious talk. That's the reality of Zoe life.

COMING TO YOUR SENSES

The story of the Prodigal Son takes a turn when the young man finds himself in a pigpen, starving, desperate. The Bible says he "came to himself" (Luke 15:17). That's the King James way of saying he came to his senses.

He woke up to reality. He saw his condition clearly for the first time. And in that moment of clarity, he made a decision that would save his life.

The father said, "This my son was dead, and is alive again." Dead. Not struggling. Not lost. Not confused. Dead. That's God's assessment of every person without Christ.

And just as physical death separates body from soul, spiritual death separates the human spirit from God. You can be walking, talking, working, achieving, and still be dead on the inside. You can have all the trappings of success and still be empty at the core.

This is the universal problem. Every human being born into this world after Adam's fall enters life spiritually dead. We have bios (biological life). We have psuche (soul life). But we don't have Zoe until we're connected to the Source of that life through Jesus Christ.

YOU MUST BE BORN AGAIN

Jesus told Nicodemus, a religious leader who had everything figured out intellectually, "Ye must be born again" (John 3:7).

Not "it would be nice if you were born again." Not "consider being born again." Must. It's not optional. It's not one path among many. It's the only way to receive Zoe life.

Nicodemus was confused. "How can a man be born when he is old? Can he enter the second time into his mother's womb, and be born?"

Jesus answered, "That which is born of the flesh is flesh; and that which is born of the Spirit is spirit" (John 3:6). Your first birth gave you biological life and soul life. But it didn't give you spiritual life. That only comes through a second birth, a spiritual birth, a supernatural birth from above.

WHAT REALLY HAPPENS AT SALVATION

So what actually happens when someone is born again? This is critical because many believers are confused about this.

When you receive Christ, your spirit, which was dead toward God, is made alive. It's regenerated, recreated, born anew. God's life (Zoe) is imparted to your human spirit. You become a new creation. "Therefore if any man be in Christ, he is a new creature: old things are passed away; behold, all things are become new" (2 Corinthians 5:17).

This is not self-improvement. It's not turning over a new leaf. It's not behavior modification. It's death and resurrection. The old you dies. The new you comes alive. Your spirit, which was separated from God, is now united with Him.

Paul describes it like this: "But he that is joined unto the Lord is one spirit" (1 Corinthians 6:17). One spirit. Not two separate spirits cooperating. One. Fused. United. Christ's life becomes your life.

So, what does this mean practically? When you were born again, you didn't just receive forgiveness of sins. You received a complete package—a full inheritance. Identity, authority, access. Every spiritual blessing in heavenly places. God gave you everything.

But here's what many believers miss: You can receive everything and still live like you have nothing.

I recently heard a story that captures this perfectly.

A young woman and her cousin stayed in a luxury penthouse suite in Bali, a booking transferred to them by a family friend who couldn't go. But they were broke students from London, so they went into full survival mode. "Don't touch anything," she told her cousin. "We can't afford this hotel."

They ate outside every meal. They lived off the complimentary breakfast, even saving bread to eat with Coke during the day. They were terrified of the costs.

On their last night, they finally ate at the hotel restaurant. When the bill came, the waiter said, "You don't need to pay. You have points."

"What points?"

He explained that the penthouse booking came with thousands of points for food, room service, car rides, massages—everything. The entire week's worth of amenities they'd been avoiding was already included in the booking.

They started ordering everything. The next day at checkout, the staff said, "You still have points. What do you want to do with them?" They ordered more food. The points were so abundant they couldn't use them all before leaving.

As she walked out, she realized: They'd spent the entire week living like paupers in a penthouse, not knowing they didn't have to. And she heard it in her spirit: "Imagine being blessed and not knowing it."

That's the reality many believers live in. They're born again. They have the new creation. They have everything. But they live beneath it because no one told them what they received.

You can be blessed and not know it. You can have access and never use it. You can be a new creation but still live from your old identity, simply because revelation is what unlocks access.

That's why you must be born again. And that's why you must understand what being born again actually means.

THE VICE PRINCIPAL'S CONVERSATION

Let me tell you about a conversation I had that brought this home for me. I was talking with the vice principal of our school, a wonderful woman, very religious, very dedicated. She asked me about my ministry, and I shared about preaching the gospel and seeing people come to Christ.

She looked at me thoughtfully and said, "You know, I've been a Christian all my life. I was raised in the church. I go every Sunday. But I'm not sure I've ever had that moment you're describing, that born-again experience."

Her honesty struck me. Here was someone who had been in church for decades, who was a good person, who believed in God, but who was uncertain whether she'd actually been born again.

I asked her, "Have you ever personally invited Jesus Christ into your heart as your Lord and Savior? Have you ever confessed your sins to Him and asked Him to save you?"

She shook her head slowly. "No. I don't think I have. I've always assumed that because I was raised in church and believed in God, I was saved."

Right there in her office, I had the privilege of leading her in a prayer of salvation. She confessed Jesus as Lord, asked Him to save her, and received Him into her heart. And when she opened her eyes, there were tears streaming down her face.

"I feel different," she said. "Something just changed inside me."

What changed? She had moved from religion to relationship. From church attendance to Christ indwelling. From spiritual death to spiritual life. She had been born again.

NOT WHO YOU USED TO BE

If you're born again, you are not the same person you were before. This is not positive thinking or self-affirmation. This is biblical reality.

The Bible doesn't say, "Try to be new." It says you ARE new. "If any man be in Christ, he is a new creature" (2 Corinthians 5:17). Present tense. Accomplished fact.

Your spirit has been recreated. You have God's nature. You have His life. You have His DNA, if you will. You're not merely forgiven; you're transformed. You are not declared righteous in name alone; you have been made righteous in reality.

This is why the devil fights so hard to keep you ignorant of this truth. If you knew who you really are, and understood what happened to you at salvation, you would live differently. You would pray differently. You would face trials differently. You would resist temptation differently.

John 1:12 says, "But as many as received him, to them gave he power to become the sons of God, even to them that believe on his name."

Notice it says "power to become," not power to try, not power to work toward, but power to BECOME. It's an accomplished reality, not an ongoing struggle.

When you received Christ, you received the power, the authority, the right, and the capacity to be a son or daughter of God. Not to try to earn that status. Not to work toward that position. To BE it. To become it instantly, completely, irrevocably.

THE INVITATION

Maybe as you're reading this, you realize you're like that vice principal. You've been in church. You believe in God. You're a good person. But you've never actually been born again. You've never personally invited Jesus into your heart.

Or maybe you've walked away from God, and you know you need to come back. Like the Prodigal Son, you need to come to your senses and return to the Father.

The good news is that the Father is waiting. He's not angry. He's not disappointed. He's watching for you, ready to run to you, ready to embrace you, ready to restore you.

Salvation is not complicated. It's not about religious rituals or church membership. It's about a simple, sincere transaction with God.

The Bible says, "If thou shalt confess with thy mouth the Lord Jesus, and shalt believe in thine heart that God hath raised him from the dead, thou shalt be saved" (Romans 10:9).

If you want to receive Zoe life today, if you want to move from spiritual death to spiritual life, you can pray something like this:

"Father God, I come to You in the name of Jesus. I confess that I am a sinner and that I need a Savior. I believe that Jesus Christ is Your Son, that He died on the cross for my sins, and that You raised Him from the dead. I ask You to forgive me of all my sins. Jesus, I receive You into my heart as my Lord and Savior. I surrender my life to You. Thank You for saving me. Thank You for giving me eternal life. In Jesus' name, Amen."

If you prayed that prayer with a sincere heart, something just happened in your spirit. You were born again. Zoe life, the very life of God has been imparted to you. You are now a new creation.

Welcome to the family of God.

CHAPTER 2 DECLARATIONS

"Dead Man Walking: The Need for New Birth"

1. I was once dead in trespasses and sins, but now I am alive with the life of God through Jesus Christ.
2. I have been born again, not improved, not renovated, but completely recreated with God's nature inside me.
3. When Christ died, I died. When He was buried, I was buried. When He rose, I rose to newness of life.
4. I am not the same person I was before salvation. The old me was executed, and the new me was created in righteousness and true holiness.
5. I have been given the power to become a son or daughter of God. This is my accomplished reality, not my ongoing struggle.
6. I am no longer a slave to sin. I am dead to sin and alive to God through Jesus Christ my Lord.
7. Because I have Jesus, I possess something that transcends death itself. I will reign with Him forever.

3

CRUCIFIED YET ALIVE

"I am crucified with Christ: nevertheless I live; yet not I, but Christ liveth in me: and the life which I now live in the flesh I live by the faith of the Son of God, who loved me, and gave himself for me." (Galatians 2:20)

This verse is one of the most revolutionary statements in all of Scripture. Read it slowly. Let it sink in. Because if you can grasp what Paul is saying here, your entire Christian experience will shift from struggle to victory, from defeat to dominance, from religious effort to supernatural rest.

Paul makes three declarations that seem to contradict each other:

- First, he says, "I am crucified." Dead. Past tense. It's done.
- Second, he says, "Nevertheless I live." Alive. Present tense. It's happening.
- Third, he says, "Yet not I, but Christ liveth in me." Not me living, but Christ living.

How can you be dead and alive at the same time? How can you be living, yet not you living? This is the mystery and the miracle of the Christian life. And until you understand it, you'll keep trying to live for God in your own strength, and you'll keep coming up short.

THE GREAT EXCHANGE

Here's what happened at the cross of Jesus Christ: There was an exchange. A divine transaction. A supernatural swap.

The old you, the person you were before Christ, with all your sin, guilt, shame, brokenness, and depravity; that person was crucified with Jesus. When He died, you died. When He was buried, you were buried. When He rose, you rose. But the person who rose is not the same person who died.

"Know ye not, that so many of us as were baptized into Jesus Christ were baptized into his death? Therefore we are buried

with him by baptism into death: that like as Christ was raised up from the dead by the glory of the Father, even so we also should walk in newness of life." (Romans 6:3-4)

Notice the language: baptized into His death, buried with Him, raised with Him. This is co-crucifixion. Co-burial. Co-resurrection.

At salvation, you received more than forgiveness. Forgiveness is wonderful, but it's not enough. You got replaced. The old you was executed. The new you was created.

2 Corinthians 5:17 doesn't say, "If any man be in Christ, he is an improved version of himself." It says, "Therefore if any man be in Christ, he is a new creature: old things are passed away; behold, all things are become new."

New creature. Not renovated. Not rehabilitated. New. Brand new. A new species of being that never existed before. A human being indwelt by the Spirit of God, carrying the Zoe life of the Creator in their recreated spirit.

RECKONING YOURSELF DEAD

Paul says in Romans 6:11, "Likewise reckon ye also yourselves to be dead indeed unto sin, but alive unto God through Jesus Christ our Lord."

The word "reckon" means to count, to consider, to acknowledge as fact. It's an accounting term. When you reckon something, you're not trying to make it true, you're accepting that it's already true and acting accordingly.

This is crucial because the devil will try to convince you otherwise. He'll point to your failures and say, "See? You're not dead to sin. You're not a new creation. Nothing really changed." And if you believe that lie, you'll live accordingly.

But God says, "Reckon yourself dead." Count it as true. Accept it as fact. Your old self died with Christ. That's not positive thinking, it's biblical reality. The question is not whether it's true. The question is whether you believe it and live from it.

NOT I, BUT CHRIST

Look again at Galatians 2:20: "yet not I, but Christ liveth in me."

This is the secret to the Christian life: It's not you trying to live for Christ. It's Christ living through you. You're not the source, you're the vessel. You're not the power, you're the channel. You're not generating the life, you're releasing the life that's already there.

For years, I tried to live the Christian life in my own strength. I would pray, "Lord, help me to be more patient.

Help me to love difficult people. Help me to overcome this temptation." And I meant well. But I was operating from the wrong paradigm.

The Christian life is not you plus Jesus doing your best together. It's Jesus living His life through you as you yield to Him. It's not "I'll try harder and God will give me a boost." It's "I can't do this, but Christ in me can, so I'm going to let Him."

Paul discovered this and declared it boldly: "I am crucified with Christ: nevertheless I live; yet not I, but Christ liveth in me." The I that lives is not the old I. It's the new I empowered by Christ.

FROM FIGHTING TO RESTING

Here's what changes when you understand this truth: You stop fighting and start resting.

The Christian life is not a constant battle to be good enough. It's not gritting your teeth and trying harder. It's learning to rest in what Christ has already done and who He's already made you to be.

Jesus said, "Come unto me, all ye that labour and are heavy laden, and I will give you rest" (Matthew 11:28). Most Christians are exhausted because they're trying to do in their own strength what only Christ can do through them.

Think about it: Can you make yourself more righteous? No. Christ is your righteousness. Can you generate more holiness? No. He is your holiness. Can you produce the fruit of the Spirit? No. The Spirit produces the fruit as you abide in Him.

Your job is not to manufacture spiritual life. Your job is to yield to the life that's already in you.

THE REALITY OF YOUR NEW IDENTITY

When you were born again, God gave you more than a second chance. He gave you a new identity. You became someone you had never been before. The Bible gives us dozens of identity statements about who we are in Christ. You are:

- A new creation (2 Corinthians 5:17)
- The righteousness of God in Christ (2 Corinthians 5:21)
- More than a conqueror (Romans 8:37)
- A saint, a holy one (Ephesians 1:1)
- Seated with Christ in heavenly places (Ephesians 2:6)
- Complete in Him (Colossians 2:10)

These are not aspirations. They're declarations. Not what you're trying to become, but what you already are in Christ.

The enemy wants to keep you ignorant of your identity because if you knew who you really are, you'd live differently. You'd pray differently. You'd face trials differently. You'd resist temptation differently.

LIVING FROM THE LIFE

So how do you practically live from this crucified-yet-alive reality?

First, you remind yourself daily of who you are. You don't wake up and try to become righteous. You wake up and remind yourself that you ARE righteous in Christ. You don't strive to be loved. You rest in the fact that you're already loved.

Second, you yield to the Holy Spirit moment by moment. When temptation comes, you stand by spiritual power, not human strength. You say, "Christ in me, live through me in this moment. I yield to Your nature, not mine."

Third, you renew your mind with the Word of God. Romans 12:2 says, "Be ye transformed by the renewing of your mind." As you meditate on Scripture, your thinking aligns with your new identity, and your behavior follows.

Fourth, you practice daily dying to self. Jesus said, "If any man will come after me, let him deny himself, and take up his cross daily, and follow me" (Luke 9:23). The cross is not a burden you carry, it's where your old self stays dead so Christ can live through you.

THE PRACTICAL QUESTION

Some will ask, "If I'm already dead to sin and alive to God, why do I still struggle? Why do I still sin?"

Because while your spirit has been completely regenerated, your mind and body are still being renewed. You have a new nature, but you still have old habits, old thought patterns, old reactions. The battlefield is in your mind.

The good news is this: The more you renew your mind to who you really are, the more your behavior will line up with your identity. You're not trying to become someone you're not. You're learning to live from who you already are.

This is the journey of sanctificationnot becoming holy, but learning to live out the holiness that's already yours in Christ. Not trying to get victory, but learning to walk in the victory that's already been won.

Galatians 2:20 is not only a nice verse to quote. It's the operational reality of your life as a believer. You have been crucified with Christ. You are nevertheless alive. And the life you now live, you live by the faith of the Son of God.

That's not aspiration. That's your address. You live there. The question is: Will you believe it and walk in it?

CHAPTER 3 DECLARATIONS

"Crucified Yet Alive"

1. I have been crucified with Christ. Nevertheless I live, yet not I, but Christ lives in me.
2. The old me died at the cross. The person who rose is not the same person who died. I am brand new.
3. I do not just reckon myself dead to sin. I know I am dead to sin and alive to God, and I live from that truth.
4. I do not generate spiritual life. Christ lives through me as I yield to Him. He is both the source and the power.
5. I stop fighting and start resting, because the Christian life is not my effort but Christ's life flowing through me.
6. I am the righteousness of God in Christ, a new creation, more than a conqueror, and complete in Him.
7. I do not strive to become holy. I learn to live out the holiness that is already mine in Christ.

4

THE BATTLE WITHIN: FLESH VS. SPIRIT

There's a war going on inside of you.

Every single day, from the moment you wake up until you lay your head down at night, a battle rages in your members. Two opposing forces are fighting for control. Two different natures are vying for dominance. Two contradictory laws are operating simultaneously.

And here's what you need to understand: The outcome of this battle determines the quality of your Christian life. It determines whether you walk in victory or defeat. It determines whether you experience the fortified life or settle for spiritual mediocrity.

Paul describes this internal warfare in Romans 8, one of the most powerful chapters in the entire Bible. But before we dive in, I need you to understand something crucial: This battle is real, but it's not equal. The flesh and the

Spirit are not evenly matched opponents. The Spirit of God in you is infinitely more powerful than the flesh. The problem is not God's powerit's our choices.

"There is therefore now no condemnation to them which are in Christ Jesus, who walk not after the flesh, but after the Spirit. For the law of the Spirit of life in Christ Jesus hath made me free from the law of sin and death." (Romans 8:1-2)

Notice two laws: the law of the Spirit of life, and the law of sin and death. Here's the good news: The law of the Spirit of life has made you FREE from the law of sin and death.

Free. Not struggling. Not barely surviving. Free.

But freedom must be walked in. Victory must be lived out. And that's what this chapter is about.

TWO LAWS OPERATING

Let me explain what Paul means by these two laws.

The law of sin and death is the principle that operates in your flesh—your unredeemed body and the patterns of your old nature. It's the gravitational pull toward selfishness, rebellion, and separation from God. It's what you inherited from Adam. It's the default setting of fallen humanity.

Before you were born again, this was the only law operating in you. You couldn't help but sin. You were a slave to it. Romans 6:17 says you were "servants of sin." Not occasional visitors to sin. Servants. Slaves. Bound.

But then something miraculous happened. You got saved. You were born again. The Spirit of God came to live inside you. And with Him came a new law—the law of the Spirit of life in Christ Jesus.

Think of it like this: Imagine you're standing at the edge of a cliff. The law of gravity is pulling you down. That's real and constant. But now imagine you have a helicopter with a powerful cable. When you attach yourself to that helicopter, you can rise above the cliff. Gravity didn't stop working, but a stronger force superseded it.

That's what happens when you walk in the Spirit. You're not trying to overcome the flesh in your own strength. You're operating by a higher law—the law of the Spirit of life—that makes you free from the law of sin and death.

But here's the critical point: You have to choose which law you're going to operate under. You have to decide which nature you're going to feed. You have to determine whether you'll walk after the flesh or after the Spirit.

THE CHOICE TO WALK

Look at verse 1 again: "who walk not after the flesh, but after the Spirit."

Notice it doesn't say "who never stumble" or "who never make mistakes." It says "who walk." Walking is continuous movement in a direction. It's your trajectory, not your occasional misstep.

To walk after the flesh means to let your unredeemed desires, appetites, and thought patterns direct your life. It means living for immediate gratification, selfish ambition, and temporal pleasure.

To walk after the Spirit means to let the Holy Spirit lead, guide, and empower your choices. It means yielding to His promptings, His wisdom, His strength.

Every day, you're walking one way or the other. Not perfectly, but directionally. The question is: Which way are you headed?

Paul elaborates on this in Galatians 5:16-17: "Walk in the Spirit, and ye shall not fulfil the lust of the flesh. For the flesh lusteth against the Spirit, and the Spirit against the flesh: and these are contrary the one to the other."

Notice the promise: "Walk in the Spirit, and ye shall not fulfil the lust of the flesh." It's not "try really hard and maybe you'll resist temptation." It's "walk in the Spirit and you WON'T fulfill the lust of the flesh." The Spirit-filled life is the victorious life.

THE MIND IS THE BATTLEGROUND

Romans 8:5-6 identifies where this battle actually takes place: "For they that are after the flesh do mind the things of the flesh; but they that are after the Spirit the things of the Spirit. For to be carnally minded is death; but to be spiritually minded is life and peace."

The battleground is your mind. What you think about determines what you walk in. What you focus on determines what you become.

If you fill your mind with fleshly things, ungodly entertainment, toxic relationships, negative thoughts, and worldly values, you will walk after the flesh. Your mind will be set on earthly things, and death, separation from God's life, will be the result.

But if you set your mind on spiritual things, the Word of God, worship, prayer, fellowship with believers, and meditating on truth, you will walk after the Spirit. And life and peace will be the result.

This is why Romans 12:2 commands us, "Be not conformed to this world: but be ye transformed by the renewing of your mind." Transformation happens in the mind. As you renew your thinking with God's Word, your behavior follows.

MORTIFYING THE DEEDS OF THE BODY

Romans 8:13 gives us a stark warning and a powerful promise: "For if ye live after the flesh, ye shall die: but if ye through the Spirit do mortify the deeds of the body, ye shall live."

The word "mortify" means to put to death. But notice, you don't do this in your own strength. You do it "through the Spirit." The Holy Spirit gives you the power to put sin to death.

This is not passive. It's not "let go and let God" while you do nothing. It's active cooperation with the Holy Spirit. You make the choice to say no to sin, and He gives you the power to follow through.

When temptation comes, and it will come, you have a choice. You can yield to the flesh, or you can yield to the Spirit. You can feed the old nature, or you can starve it. You can rehearse the lie, or you can speak the truth.

Every time you choose the Spirit over the flesh, you're mortifying the deeds of the body. You're putting sin to death. And every time you do this, it gets easier. The flesh weakens, and the Spirit strengthens.

LED BY THE SPIRIT

Romans 8:14 gives us a beautiful identity marker: "For as many as are led by the Spirit of God, they are the sons of God."

Being led by the Spirit is not mystical or complicated. It's simply this: listening to and obeying the promptings of the Holy Spirit in your daily life.

The Spirit will prompt you to pray when you'd rather scroll through your phone. He'll prompt you to forgive when you'd rather hold a grudge. He'll prompt you to speak truth when you'd rather stay silent. He'll prompt you to flee temptation when you'd rather entertain it.

These promptings are not loud and dramatic most of the time. They're gentle nudges, quiet whispers, internal convictions. But as you practice listening and obeying, you become more sensitive to His voice.

PRACTICAL STRATEGIES FOR WINNING THE BATTLE

So how do you practically walk in the Spirit and overcome the flesh? Here are some concrete strategies:

- **Start your day with God.** Before you check your phone, before you engage with the world, spend time in prayer and the Word. Set your mind on the Spirit from the beginning.
- **Starve the flesh.** Don't feed your old nature. If you struggle with lust, cut off access to pornography. If you struggle with anger, avoid situations that trigger rage. Make it harder for your flesh to act out.
- **Feed your spirit.** Whatever you feed grows. Feed your spirit with the Word, worship, prayer, and fellowship. The more you feed your spirit, the stronger it becomes.
- **Renew your mind daily.** Meditate on Scripture. Memorize verses that speak to your struggles. Replace lies with truth. Your mind is the battlefield. Win it with the Word.
- **Walk in accountability.** Don't fight alone. Have trusted believers who can speak truth into your life, who can pray with you, who can call you out when you're drifting.

- **Practice immediate obedience.** When the Spirit prompts you, obey quickly. Don't negotiate. Don't delay. Immediate obedience builds spiritual muscle.

- **Remember who you are.** You're not a slave to sin anymore. You're dead to sin and alive to God. Your identity is in Christ. Live from that truth.

The battle between flesh and Spirit is real. But the outcome is not in doubt if you're walking in the Spirit. The flesh has no chance against the power of God living in you.

Romans 8:37 declares, "Nay, in all these things we are more than conquerors through him that loved us." Not barely victorious. Not struggling survivors. More than conquerors.

That's your inheritance. That's your reality. The question is: Will you walk in it?

CHAPTER 4 DECLARATIONS

"The Battle Within: Flesh vs. Spirit"

1. The law of the Spirit of life in Christ Jesus has made me free from the law of sin and death.

2. I am not evenly matched against the flesh. The Spirit of God in me is infinitely more powerful than any fleshly desire.

3. I choose to walk after the Spirit, not after the flesh, and as I do, I will not fulfill the lust of the flesh.

4. My mind is the battleground, and I set it on things of the Spirit, bringing life, peace, and victory.

5. I mortify the deeds of the body through the Spirit, putting sin to death by His power working in me.

6. I am led by the Spirit of God, and this proves I am a child of God with authority and power.

7. I am more than a conqueror through Him who loved me, not barely victorious, but abundantly triumphant.

5

ZOE AS LIGHT: SHINING IN DARKNESS

"In him was life; and the life was the light of men. And the light shineth in darkness; and the darkness comprehended it not." (John 1:4-5)

Many think Zoe life is only about being alive. But it was never meant to stop there. Zoe life brings illumination. God does not only make you alive. He makes you a light. The life of God and the light of God are inseparable. Where there is Zoe, there is light.

And here's the powerful truth that should revolutionize how you see yourself and your purpose: You are a light-carrier. You are a darkness-dispeller. You are a beacon in a dark world.

Jesus said it plainly in Matthew 5:14: "Ye are the light of the world. A city that is set on an hill cannot be hid."

Not "you should try to be." Not "you might become." You ARE. Present tense. Current reality. If you have Zoe in you, you have light in you. And light, by its very nature, cannot be hidden.

The question is not whether you're a light. The question is whether you're shining.

DARKNESS HAS NEVER OVERCOME LIGHT

Let's revisit John 1:5: "And the light shineth in darkness; and the darkness comprehended it not."

The New International Version translates it this way: "The light shines in the darkness, and the darkness has not overcome it."

Has not overcome it. Never has. Never will. Never can.

This is one of the most foundational truths in all of Scripture, and if you can grasp it, it will change how you face every challenge, every opposition, every dark situation in your life.

Light is always stronger than darkness. Always. Without exception. Without qualification.

Think about it in physical terms. If you're in a dark room and you light a single candle, what happens? The darkness doesn't fight back. It doesn't resist. It doesn't struggle. It simply disappears. Instantly. Completely. Light always displaces darkness.

And the same is true spiritually. When the light of God enters a situation or when Zoe life shows up, darkness must flee. It has no choice. It has no power to resist. It cannot overcome light.

This means that whatever darkness you're facing right nowdepression, fear, confusion, addiction, disease, financial crisis, relational breakdownit cannot overcome the light of God in you. It might feel overwhelming. It might seem unconquerable. But that's a lie. The light in you is greater than any darkness around you.

YOU CARRY THE SOLUTION

Here's a perspective shift that changes everything: You don't go into dark situations hoping to survive. You go into them knowing you carry the solution.

The world is full of darkness. Broken marriages. Dysfunctional families. Corrupt systems. Addicted communities. Hopeless neighborhoods. And God's strategy for confronting all that darkness is not to send angels or thunder or divine interventions from heaven.

His strategy is you.

You, carrying His light. You, radiating His life. You, dispelling darkness simply by being present.

Jesus didn't say, "You might become the light of the world if you try really hard." He said, "Ye ARE the light of the world." It's your identity, not your aspiration. It's your nature, not your goal.

And the way physical light shines without effort, spiritual light flows from who you are. You do not have to manufacture it. You only have to live from your identity. The Zoe life in you naturally produces light. Your job is not to create it, but to let it shine.

LIGHT EXPOSES AND TRANSFORMS

Light does two things: it exposes and it transforms.

First, light exposes what's hidden in darkness. When you turn on a light in a dark room, you suddenly see what was there all along but couldn't be seen. Dirt. Clutter. Things out of place.

That's what happens when God's light shines in your life. It exposes sin. It reveals hidden motives. It brings secret things into the open. And that can be uncomfortable. But exposure is the first step toward transformation.

You can't deal with what you can't see. You can't fix what you don't acknowledge. Light exposes not to condemn, but to heal.

Second, light transforms. Where light shines, things change. Plants grow toward the light. Wounds heal in the light. Darkness gives way to clarity. Confusion gives way to understanding.

As you walk in the light of God's presence, as you let His Zoe life flow through you, transformation happens. Not only in you, but in the people and situations around you. Your marriage improves. Your workplace shifts. Your neighborhood changes. Light transforms everything it touches.

FROM FIGHTING TO SHINING

I'll never forget when this truth became real to me personally. For years, I found myself constantly fighting against darknessfighting against discouragement, fighting against opposition, fighting against the enemy's attacks.

And I was exhausted. Because fighting is hard. Fighting requires constant effort and energy. Fighting leaves you depleted.

But one day, the Holy Spirit showed me something: I wasn't called to fight darkness. I was called to shine light.

That changed everything. Instead of waking up ready for battle, I started waking up ready to shine. Instead of focusing on the darkness around me, I started focusing on the light within me. Instead of engaging every attack with defensive energy, I started simply being who I am—a child of light.

And you know what happened? The darkness began to flee. Not because I fought harder, but because I shined brighter.

Darkness doesn't respond to fighting. It responds to light. When light shows up, darkness has no choice but to leave.

DON'T HIDE YOUR LIGHT

Jesus continued in Matthew 5:15-16: "Neither do men light a candle, and put it under a bushel, but on a candlestick; and it giveth light unto all that are in the house. Let your light so shine before men, that they may see your good works, and glorify your Father which is in heaven."

Notice: Don't hide your light. Let it shine. Be visible. Be present. Be obvious.

Some believers try to hide their light. They're ashamed of their faith. They're intimidated by the darkness around them. They blend in, hoping not to make waves, trying not to offend.

But a hidden light serves no purpose. A lamp under a basket illuminates nothing. You were not saved to blend in. You were saved to stand out. You were not given Zoe life to keep it to yourself. You were given it to shine.

This doesn't mean being obnoxious or religious or preachy. It means being authentically who you are. It means living with integrity, speaking truth, loving genuinely, serving sacrificially, and refusing to compromise. When you do that, people notice. They can't help but see the light.

LIGHT IN THE MARKETPLACE

Your light is needed everywhere you go, not only in church, but in the marketplace. In your workplace. In your neighborhood. In your school. In your community. God didn't call you to shine only on Sundays. He called you to shine seven days a week. He called you to be light in the boardroom, in the break room, in the classroom, in the living room.

When you walk into your workplace, you're not a mere employee, you're a light-carrier. When you enter your school as student, you're also a darkness-dispeller. When you engage with your neighbors, you're not just being friendlyyou're radiating the life of God.

This means excellence in your work. Integrity in your dealings. Kindness in your interactions. Peace in your demeanor. Joy in your countenance. These are all expressions of light.

People are watching. They're looking for hope. They're searching for answers. They're desperate for light. And you carry what they need.

MAINTAINING YOUR LIGHT

While it's true that Zoe life naturally produces light, it's also true that you can dim your light through neglect or sin.

If you want to shine brightly, maintain intimacy with God. Stay in His Word. Keep your prayer life vibrant. Walk in obedience. Avoid sin that clouds your light.

Sin is like soot on a lamp. The light is still there, but it's obscured. Confess quickly. Repent immediately. Keep your lamp clean so your light can shine unhindered.

Also, guard against pride. Pride makes you think the light is yours, not His. It makes you shine on yourself rather than reflecting Him. Stay humble. Remember: You're not the light source, you're the light bearer. The light belongs to Him, and you carry it.

SHINING IN YOUR DARKEST HOUR

Sometimes the greatest test of your light comes when you face your own personal darkness. When you're going through a trial. When you're walking through a valley. When you're experiencing loss or pain.

That's when the world watches most closely. That's when your testimony is most powerful. That's when your light shines brightestnot because circumstances are bright, but because the contrast is greatest.

When you worship in the middle of your storm. When you praise in the midst of your pain. When you give thanks despite your trial. When you maintain your joy through your struggle. That's when people see that your light isn't dependent on your circumstances. It comes from within. It comes from Zoe.

And that's when your light becomes most attractive. Because everyone can shine when life is good. But shining when life is hard? That's supernatural. That's Zoe.

THE WORLD NEEDS YOUR LIGHT

Never underestimate the impact of your light. You might feel small. You might feel insignificant. You might think, "What difference can I make?"

But remember: One candle can illuminate an entire room. One star can guide a ship through the night. One light can give hope to someone in darkness.

You don't have to be a pastor or a missionary or a ministry leader to shine. Be faithful where you are. Let the life of God in you flow to those around you.

The world doesn't need more programs. It needs more light. It doesn't need more organizations. It needs more people who carry the presence of God into their everyday lives.

You are that person. You are the light of the world. Not because you're special in yourself, but because you carry the Special One inside you.

So shine. Shine in your home. Shine at your job. Shine in your community. Shine in your relationships. Let the Zoe life within you illuminate the world around you.

And as you do, watch darkness flee. Watch lives transform. Watch hope spring up. Watch glory return to the Father.

Because that's what light does. And that's who you are.

CHAPTER 5 DECLARATIONS

"Zoe as Light: Shining in Darkness"

1. I am the light of the world, not trying to become it, but living from this present reality.
2. Where I go, light goes. I carry the solution to every darkness because Zoe life produces illuminating light.
3. Darkness has never overcome light and never will. The darkness in my life, family, or circumstances cannot overcome the Zoe light in me.
4. I do not fight darkness. I shine light, and darkness must flee because it has no power against God's light.
5. I refuse to hide my light under a basket. I let it shine before others so they may see and glorify my Father in heaven.
6. I am a light carrier in the marketplace, workplace, home, and community, shining in every environment I enter.
7. Even in my darkest hour, my light shines brightest because it comes from within, from Zoe, not from my circumstances.

6

INTIMACY & POWER: LIVING IN GOD'S PRESENCE

The Christian life is not a formula. It's not a system. It's not a set of rules or a program to follow. At its core, the Christian life is a relationship. A living, breathing, moment-by-moment relationship with the living God.

And here's a secret that many believers miss: The power of God flows through intimacy with God.

You cannot manufacture spiritual power through programs, techniques, or formulas. True spiritual authority, the kind that heals the sick, casts out demons, transforms lives, and shakes nations, flows from one source: intimate relationship with the Father.

THE PRIORITY OF PRESENCE

When Mary and Martha hosted Jesus in their home, Martha was busy serving while Mary sat at Jesus' feet listening to His teaching. Martha complained, asking Jesus to tell Mary to help her. But Jesus responded with words that should arrest us: "Martha, Martha, thou art careful and troubled about many things: But one thing is needful: and Mary hath chosen that good part, which shall not be taken away from her" (Luke 10:41-42).

One thing is needful. Not many things. One thing.

Mary chose the better partsitting at His feet, being in His presence, listening to His voice. And Jesus said that would not be taken from her.

We live in a culture obsessed with productivity, efficiency, and results. Even in the church, we measure success by numbers, programs, and activities. But Jesus says there's one thing that matters most: being with Him.

If you're too busy to spend time in God's presence, you're too busy. If your schedule is so packed that you can't sit at His feet, your schedule is wrong. If your ministry activities leave no room for intimacy with God, you're doing ministry without the life of God flowing through you.

INTIMACY BIRTHS AUTHORITY

Acts 4:13 gives us a remarkable insight: "Now when they saw the boldness of Peter and John, and perceived that they were unlearned and ignorant men, they marvelled; and they took knowledge of them, that they had been with Jesus."

What gave Peter and John their authority? Not their education. Not their training. Not their credentials. They had been with Jesus.

Spending time with Jesus changes you. It transforms how you speak, how you pray, how you carry yourself. It gives you a boldness that comes not from self-confidence but from God-confidence.

The religious leaders couldn't deny the miracles. They couldn't refute the wisdom. They couldn't explain the power. All they could determine was this: These men had been with Jesus.

That's the kind of life I want to live. That's the kind of authority I want to carry. Not authority that comes from position or title or human recognition, but authority that comes from intimacy with God. Authority that makes even my opponents say, "This person has been with Jesus."

THE SECRET PLACE

Jesus modeled this for us. Despite the demands on His time, despite the crowds pressing in, despite the urgent needs surrounding Him, Jesus regularly withdrew to be alone with the Father.

Mark 1:35 tells us, "And in the morning, rising up a great while before day, he went out, and departed into a solitary place, and there prayed."

If Jesus, the Son of God, full of the Holy Spirit, walking in perfect communion with the Father needed time alone with God, how much more do we?

The secret place is where intimacy is cultivated. It's where you meet with God away from distractions, away from demands, away from the noise of life. It's where you commune with Him, listen to Him, and receive from Him.

Psalm 91:1 says, "He that dwelleth in the secret place of the most High shall abide under the shadow of the Almighty." There are blessings, protections, and provisions that only come to those who dwell in that secret place.

WHAT HAPPENS IN HIS PRESENCE

So what actually happens when you spend time in God's presence? Multiple things:

- **You are transformed.** 2 Corinthians 3:18 says we are "changed into the same image from glory to glory" as we behold the Lord. Transformation happens in His presence.
- **You receive clarity.** Confusion flees. Direction becomes clear. God's will is revealed. Light illuminates your path.
- **You gain strength.** Isaiah 40:31 promises that those who wait on the Lord shall renew their strength. His presence replenishes what life depletes.
- **You experience peace.** In His presence is fullness of joy (Psalm 16:11). Anxiety dissolves. Peace settles.
- **You receive impartation.** He downloads wisdom, revelation, strategies, and solutions. Things you couldn't figure out on your own become clear.

This is why the enemy fights so hard to keep you out of God's presence. He knows that everything changes when you meet with God.

PRAYER: THE LANGUAGE OF INTIMACY

Prayer is not a religious duty. It's the language of intimacy. It's how you communicate with the One who loves you most.

Too many believers approach prayer as a shopping list, a time to present requests and make demands. But intimacy happens when you simply talk with God. Share your heart. Listen to His. Enjoy His presence.

Yes, petition is part of prayer. But so is thanksgiving, worship, confession, and being quiet before Him.

Jesus taught His disciples to pray by giving them a model: "Our Father which art in heaven..." Notice it begins with relationship. Before requests come recognition of who He is and who you are to Him.

WORSHIP: THE PATHWAY TO INTIMACY

Worship is another gateway to intimacy. When you worship, not merely by singing songs but by pouring out your heart in adoration, something shifts. You move from the earthly realm to the heavenly realm. You step out of your circumstances and into His presence. You lift your focus from your problems to His person.

Psalm 22:3 says God inhabits the praises of His people. Where there is genuine worship, God manifests His presence.

Worship was never meant to be confined to Sundays. Let it become the rhythm of your life. Worship in your car. Worship while you work. Worship when you wake up. Worship when you're walking. Let your life be a continuous offering of praise.

THE WORD: ENCOUNTERING GOD PERSONALLY

The Bible is not a book of information. It's a book of revelation. It's how God speaks to you personally.

When you read Scripture, you're gathering knowledge. You're encountering the Living Word. Jesus Himself is called the Word (John 1:1). So when you engage with Scripture, you're engaging with Him.

Don't only read the Bible, meditate on it. Don't just study itlet it study you. Don't just memorize it, let it transform you.

As you spend time in the Word, the Holy Spirit will illuminate passages. He'll bring specific verses to your attention. He'll speak to your situation through what you're reading. That's intimacy—God speaking directly to you through His Word.

LISTENING: THE FORGOTTEN DISCIPLINE

One of the most important aspects of intimacy is also the most neglected: listening.

We're good at talking to God. We're not as good at listening to Him.

But relationship requires both speaking and listening. Imagine trying to have a friendship where you did all the talking and never listened. That wouldn't be a relationship, it would be a monologue.

God speaks. The question is: Are you listening?

He speaks through His Word. He speaks through the Holy Spirit's promptings. He speaks through circumstances. He speaks through other believers. He speaks in that still, small voice.

Learn to be still before Him. Practice silence. Wait in His presence. You'll be amazed at what you hear when you stop talking and start listening.

INTIMACY REQUIRES INTENTIONALITY

Here's the reality: Intimacy with God doesn't happen accidentally. It requires intentionality.

You have to schedule it. You have to protect it. You have to prioritize it.

Everything in your life will compete for the time you should spend with God. Work demands. Family needs. Entertainment options. Social obligations. If you wait for a convenient time, it will never come.

You have to decide: This is my time with God. This is sacred. This is non-negotiable. And then you have to guard that time fiercely.

Set a specific time. Find a specific place. Make it a habit. Because intimacy is cultivated through consistency.

THE FRUIT OF INTIMACY

When you prioritize intimacy with God, the fruit becomes evident in every area of your life.

Your prayers become more powerful. Your witness becomes more effective. Your relationships improve. Your work bears fruit. Your spiritual gifts operate more freely. Your discernment sharpens. Your joy increases. Your peace deepens.

All of this flows from intimacy. Not from trying harder or doing more, but from being with Him.

This is the fortified life. Not a life of striving and struggling, but a life rooted in relationship, flowing from presence, sustained by intimacy with the One who is Life itself.

Moses understood this. When God told him to lead Israel, Moses responded, "If thy presence go not with me, carry us not up hence" (Exodus 33:15). He was saying, "I don't want success without Your presence. I don't want achievement without intimacy. If I can't have You, I don't want anything else."

That should be our cry. Not "God, bless my plans" but "God, give me Your presence." Not "God, help me succeed" but "God, draw me close."

Because when you have His presence, you have everything. And when you walk in intimacy with Him, His power flows through you naturally.

That's the secret. That's the key. That's the fortified life.

CHAPTER 6 DECLARATIONS

"Intimacy & Power: Living in God's Presence"

1. My Christian life is not a formula or system. It is a living, breathing relationship with the living God.

2. I prioritize one thing above all else: sitting at Jesus' feet, being in His presence, and listening to His voice.

3. Intimacy with God births authority in my life. When people encounter me, they will know I have been with Jesus.

4. I dwell in the secret place of the Most High, and I abide under the shadow of the Almighty.

5. In God's presence, I am transformed. I receive clarity. I gain strength. I experience peace. I receive impartation.

6. I practice God's presence throughout my day, cultivating continuous communion with Him in all I do.

7. When I have His presence, I have everything. I choose intimacy over achievement, relationship over results.

7

LOVE IN ACTION: THE ZOE NATURE

"Beloved, let us love one another: for love is of God; and every one that loveth is born of God, and knoweth God. He that loveth not knoweth not God; for God is love." (1 John 4:7-8)

If you have Zoe life, if you've been born again and carry the life of God within you—you now have the capacity to love with God's love. Not the sentimental, emotional, conditional love of the world, but the agape love of Heaven. The self-sacrificing, unconditional, unstoppable love that defines God Himself.

And here's what many believers don't realize: Love is not a nice add-on to the Christian life. It's not optional. It's not something you can get to later after you've mastered other spiritual disciplines.

Love is the identifying mark of a Christian. It's the proof that you've been born of God. It's the evidence that Zoe life is operating in you.

LOVE IS THE IDENTIFYING MARK

Jesus made this crystal clear in John 13:34-35: "A new commandment I give unto you, That ye love one another; as I have loved you, that ye also love one another. By this shall all men know that ye are my disciples, if ye have love one to another."

Notice what He didn't say. He didn't say, "By this shall all men know you're my disciples: if you have correct theology." He didn't say, "if you attend church faithfully" or "if you know the Bible" or "if you have spiritual gifts."

He said, "if you have love one to another."

Love is the mark. Love is the sign. Love is the evidence.

You can have faith to move mountains. You can speak in tongues. You can understand all mysteries and all knowledge. But if you don't have love, Paul says, you're nothing (1 Corinthians 13:2).

This is not natural. The natural human tendency is self-preservation, self-promotion, and self-protection. But Zoe life produces a different nature, a nature that loves sacrificially, serves selflessly, and forgives freely.

LOVE AS GOD LOVED

Jesus didn't only command us to love. He showed us what love looks like. "As I have loved you, that ye also love one another."

How did Jesus love? Sacrificially. He laid down His life. Unconditionally. He loved while we were still sinners. Actively. His love was not a feeling alone. It was proven through action.

That's the standard. Not human love that fluctuates based on feelings or circumstances. God's love: consistent, committed, covenant love.

This kind of love is impossible in your own strength. You can't manufacture it through willpower or self-discipline. But it's the natural overflow of Zoe life. When God's life is flowing through you, God's love flows through you.

LOVE YOUR ENEMIES

Jesus takes it even further: "But I say unto you, Love your enemies, bless them that curse you, do good to them that hate you, and pray for them which despitefully use you, and persecute you" (Matthew 5:44).

Love your enemies. This is not natural. This is supernatural. This is Zoe.

The world says, "Love your friends and hate your enemies." Jesus says, "Love your enemies and pray for those who persecute you."

Why? "That ye may be the children of your Father which is in heaven" (Matthew 5:45). This kind of love demonstrates whose children you are. It proves you've been born of God.

When you can love someone who's hurt you, bless someone who's cursed you, and pray for someone who's persecuted you, that's not you—that's Zoe. That's the life of God operating through you.

LOVE IN THE CHURCH

If love should characterize all of life, it should especially characterize the church. The body of Christ should be the most loving community on earth.

Yet too often, it's not. Too often, churches are marked by division, gossip, criticism, and judgment. Believers attacking believers. Christians tearing each other down.

Paul addresses this in 1 Corinthians 13. Before he writes those beautiful verses about love being patient and kind, he's addressing a church full of conflict, competition, and chaos. They had spiritual gifts operating, but they didn't have love.

And God said, essentially, "What good are gifts without love? What value is there in manifestations without charity?"

We need to get this right in the church. We need to prioritize love above preferences, above traditions, above our opinions about secondary issues.

Romans 14:19 says, "Let us therefore follow after the things which make for peace, and things wherewith one may edify another." In other words: pursue what builds up, not what tears down. Pursue what unites, not what divides.

LOVE IN THE HOME

If love should mark the church, how much more should it mark your home?

Your spouse should experience God's love through you. Your children should see what unconditional love looks like because they experience it from you. Your family should be your first ministry, not an afterthought.

Ephesians 5:25 commands husbands to "love your wives, even as Christ also loved the church, and gave himself for it." That's sacrificial, servant-hearted, selfless love.

Parents, Colossians 3:21 warns, "Fathers, provoke not your children to anger, lest they be discouraged." Love doesn't provoke. Love doesn't discourage. Love builds up.

Your home should be the safest place on earth. A place where love is tangible, grace is abundant, and mercy flows freely.

LOVE IS PRACTICAL

Love is not a feeling. It's an action. James 2:15-16 makes this clear: "If a brother or sister be naked, and destitute of daily food, And one of you say unto them, Depart in peace, be ye warmed and filled; notwithstanding ye give them not those things which are needful to the body; what doth it profit?"

Faith without works is dead. Love without action is empty.

1 John 3:18 says, "My little children, let us not love in word, neither in tongue; but in deed and in truth."

So what does practical love look like?

- It helps when there's a need.
- It serves without expecting anything in return.
- It speaks words of encouragement.
- It listens with genuine interest.

- It forgives freely and quickly.
- It gives generously.
- It prays earnestly for others.
- It shows up in difficult times.

These are not extraordinary acts. They're simply love in action. And when you practice these things consistently, you demonstrate that Zoe life is real in you.

LOVE NEVER FAILS

1 Corinthians 13:8 declares, "Charity never faileth." Love never fails.

Other things will pass away. Prophecies will cease. Tongues will end. Knowledge will vanish. But love remains. Love endures. Love lasts.

Why? Because God is love. And when you love with His love, you're operating in something eternal, something unshakeable, something that cannot be defeated.

Love overcomes hate. Love conquers fear. Love bridges divides. Love heals wounds. Love transforms hearts. Love changes everything.

And the beautiful thing is this: You don't have to generate this love. You have to release it. It's already in you. Zoe life produces God's love naturally.

Romans 5:5 says, "The love of God is shed abroad in our hearts by the Holy Ghost which is given unto us." It's already there. Your job is to let it flow.

THE ULTIMATE EXPRESSION OF LOVE

The ultimate expression of love is found at the cross. "But God commendeth his love toward us, in that, while we were yet sinners, Christ died for us" (Romans 5:8).

Jesus didn't wait for us to get our act together. He didn't wait for us to become loveable. He loved us while we were still His enemies. He died for us while we were still in rebellion.

That's the love we're called to demonstrate. That's the love that flows from Zoe life.

And when the world sees that kind of love—love that serves enemies, forgives offenders, blesses persecutors, and gives without expecting return—they'll know something supernatural is at work.

They'll see that you've been with Jesus. They'll see that you carry the life of God. They'll see Zoe.

LIVING IN LOVE

So how do you live a life characterized by love?

First, stay connected to the Source. Abide in Christ. You can't give what you don't have. Spend time in His presence, receiving His love, being filled with His Spirit.

Second, practice love daily. Don't wait for grand opportunities. Love in the small moments. The everyday interactions. The mundane situations. Love is built through a thousand small acts of kindness.

Third, when you fail, and you will fail, repent quickly and start again. Love is not perfection. It's direction. Keep moving toward love, even when you stumble.

Fourth, ask the Holy Spirit to help you. When you encounter someone difficult to love, pray, "Holy Spirit, love this person through me." He will. Because love is His nature.

LOVE IS THE PROOF

At the end of the day, love is the proof that Zoe life is real. It's the evidence that you've truly been born again. It's the demonstration that God's nature is in you.

You can have all the right doctrine. You can attend every service. You can quote Scripture fluently. But if you don't love, it means nothing.

The world is watching. They're not impressed with our theology. They're not convinced by our arguments. But they can't deny love.

When they see love that mirrors Christ, love that gives without expecting return, love that forgives the unforgivable, love that serves sacrificially, that's when they believe.

That's when they say, "There must be something real here. There must be something different about these people. There must be a God who lives in them."

That's Zoe. That's the fortified life. That's the life you were created to live.

So love. Love boldly. Love radically. Love sacrificially. Love as you've been loved by God.

Because love never fails. And when you love with God's love, you're living in the fullness of the life He's given you.

CHAPTER 7 DECLARATIONS

"Love in Action: The Zoe Nature"

1. I have been born of God, and because God is love, His love flows through me to everyone I encounter.
2. Love is my identifying mark as a disciple of Jesus. By this, all people will know I belong to Him.
3. I love as Christ loved me, sacrificially, unconditionally, and actively, not just with words but with deeds and truth.
4. I love my enemies, bless those who curse me, do good to those who hate me, and pray for those who persecute me.
5. I practice love daily in my church, my home, my workplace, and my community. Love is not just a feeling but an action.
6. The love of God is shed abroad in my heart by the Holy Spirit. I do not manufacture it. I release what is already in me.
7. I walk in love because love never fails. It overcomes hate, conquers fear, bridges divides, heals wounds, and transforms hearts.

8

THE FORTIFIED DAILY LIFE: WALKING IN ZOE EVERY DAY

Knowledge without application is useless. Revelation without implementation is powerless. Understanding without action is empty.

You've journeyed through seven chapters discovering the power of Zoe life. You understand what it is. You know how you received it. You've learned about your new identity, the battle within, the light you carry, the intimacy that produces power, and the love that must flow through you.

Now comes the most important question: How do you walk this out daily?

Because the fortified life is not a destination you arrive at, it's a daily walk. It's not a one-time experience, it's a moment-by-moment choosing. It's not a theory to understand, it's a reality to live.

This final chapter is about practical application. About taking everything you've learned and translating it into everyday life.

START YOUR DAY WITH GOD

How you start your day determines how you live your day.

Before you check your phone. Before you scroll through social media. Before you dive into emails or news or the demands of the day, meet with God.

This is not legalism. It's wisdom. You're setting the tone. You're establishing your focus. You're connecting to the Source before you engage with the world.

Even if it's 15 minutes, give God the first fruits of your day. Pray. Read a passage of Scripture. Worship. Be still in His presence.

As you do this consistently, you'll notice a difference. You'll start your day from rest instead of rushing into it from anxiety. You'll have clarity instead of confusion. You'll carry peace instead of stress.

Jesus modeled this. He rose early to be with the Father. If the Son of God needed time with the Father before facing the day, how much more do we?

FEED YOUR SPIRIT, STARVE YOUR FLESH

Remember the battle between flesh and Spirit we discussed in Chapter 4? That battle is won through consistent choices about what you feed.

Whatever you feed grows. Whatever you starve shrinks.

Feed your spirit with the Word of God, worship, prayer, and fellowship with believers. The more you feed your spirit, the stronger it becomes, and the easier it is to walk in the Spirit.

Starve your flesh by removing access to things that trigger temptation. If you struggle with certain content online, install accountability software. If certain relationships pull you toward sin, create boundaries. If certain environments compromise your witness, avoid them.

This is not about becoming isolated or religious. It's about being intentional. It's about guarding the life God has given you.

PRACTICE THE PRESENCE

Brother Lawrence wrote about "practicing the presence of God," living with a constant awareness that God is with you, no matter what you're doing.

This transforms ordinary moments into sacred ones. You are not working alone. You are working with God.

You are not running errands alone. You are walking with God. You are not having conversations alone. You are representing God.

Throughout your day, cultivate awareness of His presence. Talk to Him silently as you go about your tasks. Thank Him for small blessings. Ask Him for wisdom in decisions. Acknowledge Him in all your ways.

Proverbs 3:6 promises, "In all thy ways acknowledge him, and he shall direct thy paths." This is continuous communion. This is walking in the Spirit.

GUARD YOUR MIND

The mind is the battleground, so you must guard it vigilantly.

Philippians 4:8 gives us the standard: "Finally, brethren, whatsoever things are true, whatsoever things are honest, whatsoever things are just, whatsoever things are pure, whatsoever things are lovely, whatsoever things are of good report; if there be any virtue, and if there be any praise, think on these things."

Guard what you watch. Guard what you listen to. Guard what you read. Guard what you dwell on.

When negative thoughts come, and they will come, don't entertain them. Take them captive. Replace them with truth. Speak Scripture over yourself.

2 Corinthians 10:5 says we're to cast down imaginations and bring "into captivity every thought to the obedience of Christ." This is an active process. You have authority over your thought life.

MAKE LOVE YOUR DEFAULT RESPONSE

In every interaction, in every situation, in every relationship—choose love.

When someone cuts you off in traffic, choose love. When a coworker criticizes you, choose love. When a family member disappoints you, choose love.

This doesn't mean you're a doormat. It doesn't mean you have no boundaries. It means your default response is grace, not judgment. Mercy, not condemnation. Blessing, not cursing.

Ask yourself throughout the day: What would love do in this moment? How would Jesus respond to this person? Then let the Holy Spirit love through you.

SPEAK LIFE

Proverbs 18:21 says, "Death and life are in the power of the tongue." Your words matter. Your declarations shape reality.

Stop speaking death over your circumstances. Stop declaring defeat. Stop agreeing with the enemy's narrative.

Instead, speak what God says. Declare His promises. Prophesy life over your situation.

If you are facing financial hardship, do not complain about lack. Declare, "My God supplies all my needs according to His riches in glory." If you are dealing with sickness, do not rehearse symptoms. Declare, "By His stripes I am healed." If you are experiencing relational conflict, do not vent frustration. Pray blessing over that relationship.

Your words have creative power. Use them to build, not destroy. To bless, not curse. To declare life, not death.

SERVE SOMEONE EVERY DAY

The fortified life is not self-focused. It's others-focused. You were strengthened to be a blessing.

Make it a daily practice to serve someone. Look for opportunities. Be intentional.

Buy coffee for the person behind you in line. Text an encouraging word to someone going through difficulty. Help a neighbor with yard work. Mentor someone younger in the faith.

Jesus said, "It is more blessed to give than to receive" (Acts 20:35). When you serve others, you experience the joy of being God's hands and feet.

END YOUR DAY WITH GRATITUDE

Before you go to sleep, review your day with thanksgiving.

What did God do today? How did He show up? What blessings did you experience, even small ones?

Cultivating gratitude trains your mind to see God's faithfulness. It shifts your perspective from what's lacking to what's abundant.

1 Thessalonians 5:18 says, "In every thing give thanks: for this is the will of God in Christ Jesus concerning you." Not for everything, but in everything. Even in difficult circumstances, you can find something to thank God for.

Make it a habit. Every night, list three things you're grateful for. You'll be amazed how this simple practice transforms your outlook.

WHEN YOU STUMBLE

You will have days when you don't do this perfectly. Days when you fail. Days when you stumble.

That's okay. This is not about perfection. It's about direction. It's not about never falling. It's about getting back up quickly.

When you sin, confess immediately. Don't wallow in guilt. Don't let condemnation sideline you. 1 John 1:9 promises, "If we confess our sins, he is faithful and just to forgive us our sins, and to cleanse us from all unrighteousness."

Confess. Receive forgiveness. Get back in the race.

The enemy wants you to believe that one failure means total defeat. That's a lie. The fortified life is not a life without setbacks. It's a life that keeps moving forward despite setbacks.

THE POWER OF CONSISTENCY

Small disciplines practiced consistently produce extraordinary results.

You don't transform overnight. You transform day by day. Choice by choice. Moment by moment.

Reading Scripture for 15 minutes daily. Praying for 10 minutes every morning. Speaking life instead of death. Choosing love instead of bitterness. Serving others sacrificially.

These seem small. But compounded over weeks, months, and years, they produce a life that's radically different from the norm.

Don't despise small beginnings. Don't wait until you can do something big. Start where you are. Do what you can. Be faithful in little, and God will entrust you with much.

THIS IS NOT RELIGIOUS ROUTINE

Before I close this chapter, I need to address something: These practices are not a religious checklist. They're not rules to earn God's favor. They're not laws to follow out of obligation.

They're pathways to intimacy. They're habits that cultivate relationship. They're disciplines that position you to receive from God and flow in His life.

You don't do these things to become spiritual. You do them because you ARE spiritual. You don't practice them to get God to love you. You practice them because He already loves you and wants to fellowship with you.

This is grace-empowered living. Not law-based striving. You're not trying to earn what you already have. You're learning to live from what you've already received.

CHAPTER 8 DECLARATIONS

"The Fortified Daily Life: Walking in Zoe Every Day"

1. I start my day with God, setting my mind on Him before engaging with the world, establishing peace and clarity from the beginning.

2. I feed my spirit daily with God's Word, worship, prayer, and fellowship, starving my flesh and strengthening my spirit.

3. I practice the presence of God throughout my day, maintaining continuous communion with Him in every task and conversation.

4. I guard my mind, taking every thought captive and thinking on things that are true, honest, just, pure, lovely, and of good report.

5. I make love my default response in every interaction, choosing grace over judgment, mercy over condemnation, and blessing over cursing.

6. I speak life over my circumstances, declaring God's promises and prophesying victory—my words have creative power.

7. I walk in consistency, not perfectionwhen I stumble, I confess quickly, receive forgiveness, and keep moving forward in Zoe life.

CONCLUSION

WHERE YOU'RE GOING

You've come to the end of this book, but this is the beginning of your journey.

Everything you have learned about Zoe life, about your new identity, about the battle within, about shining as light, about intimacy and power, about walking in love, and about daily practices is preparation for the life God has called you to live.

You're not meant to merely survive. You're meant to thrive. You are not meant to get by. You are meant to overflow. You're not meant to live in defeat. You're meant to walk in victory.

This is the fortified life. A life rooted in God's presence. A life empowered by His Spirit. A life flowing with His love. A life radiating His light. A life making a difference in the world.

The world is waiting. People need what you carry. They need the hope you have. They need the light you shine. They need the love you demonstrate.

Go forth in confidence. Not confidence in yourself, but confidence in the One who lives in you.

You are not alone. You are not weak. You are not insufficient.

You have Zoe, the very life of God dwelling in your spirit.

And that changes everything.

YOUR DAILY DECLARATION

Here's a declaration you can speak over yourself each morning:

I am alive with the life of God. I am a new creation. The old me is dead; the new me is alive in Christ. I have been crucified with Christ, nevertheless I live—yet not I, but Christ lives in me. I am dead to sin and alive to righteousness.

I am a child of God, filled with His Spirit, empowered by His grace. I am the light of the world. Darkness cannot overcome me. I walk by the Spirit, not by the flesh. I am more than a conqueror.

I am loved unconditionally. I am forgiven completely. I am strengthened daily. The law of the Spirit of life has made me free from the law of sin and death.

I dwell in the secret place of the Most High. Intimacy with God produces authority in my life. I walk in love because God is love and His love flows through me.

Today, I will shine. Today, I will love. Today, I will serve. Today, I will walk in victory. Because Zoe, the very life of God, is in me.

In Jesus' name, Amen.

www.ingramcontent.com/pod-product-compliance
Lightning Source LLC
LaVergne TN
LVHW010935110826
845149LV00013B/2618
9781965593790